239 Questions to Ask Before Marriage

Things Couples Should Talk About While Preparing for Marriage (Conversation Starters)

By

Claire Robin

239 Questions to Ask Before Marriage

First edition. April, 2018.

Copyright © 2018 Claire Robin

Written by Claire Robin

<u>Other Books by the Same Author</u>

I want to thank you for purchasing this book. Below are other books that will also help in boosting intimacy and improving your marriage positively:

1. <u>200 Ways to Seduce Your Husband:</u> How to Boost Your Marriage Libido and Actually Enjoy Sex: A Couple's Intimacy Guide

2. <u>232 Questions for Couples</u>: Romantic Relationship Conversation Starters for Connecting, Building Trust, and Emotional Intimacy

3. <u>Communication in Marriage:</u> How to Communicate Effectively With Your Spouse, Build Trust and Rekindle Love

4. <u>Anger Management in Marriage:</u> Ways to Control Your Emotions, Get Healed of Hurts & Respond to Offenses (Overcome Bad Temper)

5. <u>100 Ways to Cultivate Intimacy in Your Marriage</u>: How to Improve Communication, Build Trust and Rekindle Love

6. <u>40 Bible Verses to Pray Over Your Husband and Marriage:</u> Powerful Scriptural Prayers for Protection, Guidance, Wisdom, Companionship, Commitment, Healing, and Deliverance

7. <u>Sexual Intimacy in Marriage:</u> 100 Facts Nobody Ever Told You About Sex and Romance [FREE ON KINDLE]

8. <u>How to Build Trust in a Relationship:</u> Powerful Ways to Rebuild Effective Communication, Resolve Conflict, Improve Intimacy, And Avoid Betrayal

9. <u>How to Deal with Husband's Pornography Addiction:</u> Powerful Ways To Help Your Spouse To Overcome & Recover Completely, While Improving Your Sexual Intimacy

15. <u>Surviving an Abusive Relationship:</u> How to Deal with Verbal, Emotional & Physical Abuse in A Relationship

Table of Contents

Introduction

Asking the right questions is the only way to know if you are with the right person or not. Unfortunately, most people fail to ask the right questions before marriage, and only tend to figure out some of the things missing after they have tied the knot. The purpose of this book is to bring to light some of the right questions to ask in order to know your boyfriend or girlfriend better. Asking this questions will help you know this person and to determine whether this is the one or not. Without getting distracted by other qualities that make your partner attractive, you will have a better outlook of the meaning of your relationship and how you could grow with this person. Also, without fear, you will prove your compatibility. If your partner while dating is not afraid of answering all these questions, then they won't be afraid to answer any other question even when you get married. These questions may serve as prove, or a measuring scale, to determine the extent of understanding you have for each other and to know the kind of direction you should take your relationship. The satisfaction driven form the entire committed relationship will be determined by how better the partners communicate. These questions and conversation starters will help you communicate better even as you take the advantage to get to know this person better at a little amount of time.

CHAPTER ONE: Before Engagement

1. How would you deal with a disagreement between me and your family members?

2. Who would you defend first?

3. Would you take sides?

4. How would you deal with sickness? What does a long-term sickness mean to your commitment?

5. What do you feel about divorce?

6. Do you think people with kids should divorce?

7. Can people in love still divorce?

8. What is your point of satisfaction? Emotionally, physically or sexually?

9. What extent would you go to make sure we eat?

10. Do you think male and female should have specific separate roles in marriage?

11. How would you delegate responsibilities between us?

12. What would be the worst news as a married person?

13. What do you think about DNA tests for kids?

14. How would you deal with critical sickness in children? What would be your reaction?

15. How would you deal with debt?

16. Would pre-marriage debt become a concern of yours?

17. Do you think debt is a way of life? Would you run a family like a country?

18. Do you have any debt as we speak?

19. Do you think credit cards should exist at all?

20. Would you still use credit card if you have options not to?

21. What is your ideal wedding?

22. What is your ideal saving plan?

23. What kind of account system do you prefer? Single account? Double account? Single and double?

24. Would you rather spend everything or save some for the rainy day?

25. What is your opinion about babysitters?

26. What is your ideal holiday plan?

27. Would you stay at home for the kids if my work would consume most of my time?

28. Would you hang out with couples' friends or friends who are still single?

29. When would you resort to marriage counselling?

30. Who would you communicate about marital problems apart from me?

31. With kids and everything, how many times a month would you have date nights?

32. How do you picture yourself as a dad?

33. Are you the disciplinary or mild dad?

34. Would you employ someone to do the house chores? In what circumstance?

35. List some of your family members you would like to take in, if anything bad would happen.

36. Would you feel comfortable about me taking in other family members?

37. What is your ideal form of retirement?

38. Do you have a plan in mind about retirement?

39. Where would you live on retiring?

40. How many kids would you like to have?

41.Do you care more about the gender?

CHAPTER TWO: Before Moving in Together

1. Are you considering our relationship to be marriage oriented?

2. Would you have a problem with me working late?

3. Would you pick up the slack if I have to work late?

4. How much time would you like alone, even when we live together?

5. Who would you prefer to be the third person in our home, considering different circumstances?

6. Are you a pet lover? Would you like to have one in the future when we are staying together?

7. Are you a hoarder or a neat freak?

8. How would you delegate house chores?

9. For how long are you planning to date before getting married?

10. How do we share bills?

11. Who would own the house?

12. How would we share things in case of break up?

13. What exactly are you ready for?

14. How do you feel about us living together?

15. Do you think it's a step further towards increased commitment?

CHAPTER THREE:
Intense Questions

1. What do you think about flirting?

2. Would you flirt with my friends?

3. How would you describe me to your friends?

4. Would you spend more time with my family members? How much time?

5. What is the best way to deal with conflict between a family member and your wife/husband?

6. What do you think about this my friend or family member?

7. If one of your family members doesn't like me, would you break up?

8. Would you give another girl your number?

9. Would you flirt back with a stranger?

10. In 4 years, where would you want to see us?

11. How would you handle long-term relationship?

12. How would you handle long-distance relationship?

13. Would you leave your job to move with me to a city, if I had a better job?

14. How comfortable are you talking about the progress of our relationship?

15. Do you consider finding emotional refuge with the opposite sex as cheating?

16. What is your ideal definition of cheating?

17. What do you think about divorce?

18. What first come to mind when you hear the word marriage?

19. What first comes to mind when the word 'separation' is mentioned?

20. Did you ever break up with someone you thought you were going to spend a lifetime with?

21. How did you handle the separation?

22. How would you handle separation this time?

23. What did you learn about committed relationship from your recent breakup?

24. How would you initiate a breakup?

25. Would you complain about me to your friends or families?

26. Would you support my career to every extent?

27. Do you think my success will affect our relationship to a certain level?

28. Would you still be comfortable if when I become________?

29. What is your ultimate rule for cultivating a healthy relationship?

30. What is the best secret you've ever known for maintaining a long-term relationship?

31. Which one would you apply to make sure that our relationship grows to the utmost?

32. How important is loyalty to you compared to exclusivity in your relationship?

33. Does your commitment depend on feelings or the legal obligation of marriage and togetherness?

34. What is this one thing I would do that will shake down the trust you have for me?

35. Would you be comfortable if I have a coffee with someone of an opposite sex?

36. How comfortable would you be about a friend of the opposite sex?

37. What was your best moment of control? When did you handle conflict like a boss?

38. Would you prefer to travel all the time or just stay in a single town?

39. On the scale of 1 – 10, rate your anger control skill.

40. What are your rules for money management?

41. If you would lose your job, what would be your first resort?

42. When was the most memorable moment you broke the law?

43. Can you think of the worst thing you have ever done with your friend?

44. Would you do that if given the same circumstance or opportunity?

45. How would you handle stress and pressure?

46. What is your top 3 bad habits?

47. Have you tried improving? What is your weakness when it comes to change?

48. "What would you be your ultimate response when someone is hitting on me?"

49. How do you feel about testing for STDs?

50. Have you ever been tested with another partner?

51. What was the riskiest thing you've ever did that almost exposed you to STD?

52. How many people have you been intimate with?

53. How do you feel about your ex?

54.Do you think you make the right choice by letting go of your past relationship?

CHAPTER FOUR: Fun Questions

1. If you would receive a call that you won 1 million dollars, where would be your first stop?

2. How would you caution me if my hair is not standing well?

3. "If you are to measure the time you spend online, how much time do you spend on Facebook?"

4. What is your favorite song of the year?

5. What was the book you read that changed a lot about how you see the society?

6. Did you read any novel that painted the way you want your love life to be?

7. Who is your favorite actor?

8. Who is your favorite writer?

9. Do you like rap music?

10.If you were to choose one rapper, who would you like to hang out with?

11. Would you laugh at my joke when no one else would?

12. Do you hate a particular house chore?

13. What would you be doing with your free time if you are to stay at home?

14. What's one thing that almost everyone knows how to do very well and you are terrible at?

15. What language would you prefer to speak apart from English?

16. Tea or coffee?

17. Sugar or honey?

18. What is your ideal meal of the day?

19. Would you prefer to use Google Map or ask strangers directions?

20. Who is your favorite player?

21. "What's one sport you can't stand to watch?"

22. What would be your favorite thing to do to relieve stress?

23. How do I contribute into making you feel good if you had a stressful day?

24. Is this your dream job?

25. To what extent would you go to achieve your dream job?

26. Do you still hope to achieve your dream?

27. Did you get disappointed when you visited the city you always admire through pictures?

28. Would you kiss me on the bus?

29. If you were given a chance to call me a funny name, what would you call me?

30. Do you have a celebrity crush?

31. On a scale of 1 – 10, how superstitious are you?

32. Would you be anyone else?

33. If you were given a day to become the president of your country, what would you change?

34. What is your favorite color?

35. What is one thing you are ashamed of that you love dearly?

36. What is one embarrassing moment you'd never forget?

37. Would you eat any type of meat?

38. Have you ever eaten anything and regretted?

39. What is the one thing that made us compatible?

40. What is the one thing we have in common that seems like we've known each other forever?

41. What is one object that reminds you of me?

42. What is one thing you'd always be proud of about your achievements?

43. What is the thing you are proud of about your physical appearance?

44. What makes you confidence about the person you are right now?

45. Would you be comfortable shopping with me if I have to buy dresses and undies?

46. What is the one word that describes our relationship?

47. What is the one word that describes me?

48. What game would you like to play with me?

CHAPTER FIVE: Going Personal

1. Who among your parents did you admire the most when growing up?

2. "What was your favorite summer vacation as a kid?"

3. As a kid, were you an introvert, extrovert or somewhere in-between?

4. Did you have a pet when you were growing up?

5. What skill did you regret not having as a kid?

6. Did anything happen that changed who you are?

7. How close are you to your other family members?

8. Did someone outside your family do something that you can't forget? Something nice?

9. What was the sacrifice you made for the sake of your parents' happiness you would never forget?

10.Did you have a favorite subject?

11. Who was your favorite teacher at school?

12. What is the one thing you can remember about school that made your childhood awesome?

13. Did you break the law in school?

14. Did you become a hero about something in your class or school?

15. What was the form of parenthood you grew up in? Was there any form of equality?

16. Was your parent's relationship awesome?

17. What would you change about your parent's relationship in your own case?

18. What is your originality?

19. What would you like to be identified by?

20. How many cities have you lived in, while growing up?

CHAPTER SIX: Before The Marriage

1. Do you think your past can disturb the peace of our marriage?

2. What is the one thing you are afraid of in the future?

3. How would you deal with responsibilities, especially when they become overwhelming?

4. How would you deal with grief?

5. How do you cope with lack of sleep?

6. How do you cope with family stress?

7. What would you resort to, in cases of job loss?

8. What is the one biggest way you can think of, to express your love in our marriage?

9. How long would you do that?

10. How often do you think communication is important to building a better relationship?

11. What is the one tip for a great marriage?

12. Would you like a stay at home wife or a career woman?

13. Do you prefer babysitters or sitting at home to take care of kids on your own?

14. What are the top 3 reasons to be married?

15. Have you ever had a drinking problem?

16. What do you think is the normal phase for drinking?

17. Have you ever dealt with money issues? Debt?

18. How important is sex to you?

19. How significant is faithfulness to your happiness?

20. Are you comfortable with drastic change? Are you ready for change?

21. Would you still live in the city when you retire?

22. How significant is religion or faith to you in your daily dealings and endeavors?

23. Do you live by faith?

24. How many kids would you like to have?

25. Would you like to have kids immediately after we get married?

CHAPTER SEVEN: When You Are Still Dating

1. How close are you with your siblings?

2. Do you like your parents' relationship? What would you integrate into your relationship?

3. Who is your celebrity crush?

4. What would you do that is less manly or womanly, just out of love?

5. Do you have any regrets?

6. Do you have any secret that you
   would like to share only with the
   ones you love?

7. Are you afraid of being judged or
   criticized when people know some
   things about you?

8. What is the one thing you would
   change about you?

9. What is your best fear?

10. What is your ideal adventure?

11. Do you have any fantasy?

12. When you first saw me, what was
    your first impression?

13. What is the one thing you have done in the past that you are still proud of?

14. Did you make an unusual breakthrough as a kid?

15. What is your relationship like with your ex?

16. Why did you end your last relationship? Whose fault did you think was it?

17. What is your definition of a perfect relationship?

18. When was your first heartbreak?

19.Is this the first time you've been in

love?

CHAPTER EIGHT:
Bonus: Questions to Ask
On a First Date

1. When do you find yourself planning?

2. Do you think planning is very important when it comes to how to start a relationship?

3. What is your favorite pet?

4. Do you love ice cream? What is your ideal flavor?

5. How often people become kind to you?

6. What is your craziest fantasy?

7. If you were allowed to choose an adventure? What would you like to do on your next vacation?

8. Who is your favorite artist?

9. Who is the one famous person you would like to hang out with? Why?

10. Are you a movie or a music person?

11. What song would you sing without missing the lyrics?

12. What are your best wishes about relationship?

13. Did you do anything recently that impressed everyone?

14. What is your dream job?

15. Did your ambition changed as you were growing up?

16. What is your biggest weakness?

17. What is the one thing almost everyone does that you think is totally lame?

Other Books by the Same Author

1. <u>200 Ways to Seduce Your Husband:</u> How to Boost Your Marriage Libido and Actually Enjoy Sex: A Couple's Intimacy Guide

2. <u>232 Questions for Couples</u>: Romantic Relationship Conversation Starters for Connecting, Building Trust, and Emotional Intimacy

3. <u>Communication in Marriage:</u> How to Communicate Effectively With Your Spouse, Build Trust and Rekindle Love

4. <u>Anger Management in Marriage:</u> Ways to Control Your Emotions, Get Healed of Hurts & Respond to Offenses (Overcome Bad Temper)

5. <u>100 Ways to Cultivate Intimacy in Your Marriage</u>: How to Improve

Communication, Build Trust and
Rekindle Love

6. 40 Bible Verses to Pray Over Your
Husband and Marriage: Powerful
Scriptural Prayers for Protection,
Guidance, Wisdom, Companionship,
Commitment, Healing, and Deliverance

7. Sexual Intimacy in Marriage: 100
Facts Nobody Ever Told You About Sex
and Romance [FREE ON KINDLE]

8. How to Build Trust in a Relationship:
Powerful Ways to Rebuild Effective
Communication, Resolve Conflict,
Improve Intimacy, And Avoid Betrayal

9. How to Deal with Husband's
Pornography Addiction: Powerful Ways
To Help Your Spouse To Overcome &
Recover Completely, While Improving
Your Sexual Intimacy

10. How to Deal with A Difficult Spouse:
Regain Control, Living with a